Healing with Angels

MESSENGERS OF HOPE

Randy Petersen

Publications International, Ltd.

Randy Petersen is the author of *Why Me, God?*; *The Path to Heaven*; and *The Powerful Prayer of Jabez*. He earned a B.A. in ancient languages from Wheaton College before becoming executive editor of *Bible Newsletter* and other publications. Now a full-time freelance writer and editor, he has also contributed to more than 20 other books, such as *The Revell Bible Dictionary* and *The Christian Book of Lists*, and to a wide variety of magazines, such as *Christian History*.

Acknowledgments:

Unless otherwise noted, all scripture quotations are taken from the *New Revised Standard Version* of the Bible. Copyright © 1989 by the Division of Christian Education of the National Council of the Churches of Christ in the USA. Used by permission. All rights reserved.

Scripture quotations marked KJV are taken from *The Holy Bible, King James Version.*

Scripture quotations marked NIV are taken from *The Holy Bible, New International Version.* Copyright © 1973, 1978, 1984, International Bible Society. Used by permission of Zondervan Publishing House. All rights reserved.

Scripture quotations marked NLT are taken from *The Holy Bible, New Living Translation.* Copyright © 1996. Used by permission of Tyndale House Publishers, Inc. All rights reserved.

Cover Photos: **PhotoDisc**

Contents

Finding Help for Feeling Better

God's Healing Power

We try to take care of ourselves. If we feel a new twinge or develop an ache that surprises us, we'll take a vitamin or cook up some chicken soup. *That ought to take care of it,* we think. And sometimes it does.

The ache we feel may be heartache. We might lose a dear family member, or perhaps we are touched by divorce. There are other possibilities, as well. People change jobs and move far away. Misunderstandings make enemies of long-term friends. Many of us get depressed about the steady steps of the aging process. Whatever the case, we feel a sense of loss, and we're not sure what to do about that.

I can handle this, we tell ourselves. *It's just a bad mood, a bad day, a bad break.* We like to think we can quickly get back to normal. We can save ourselves. The whole "self-help" industry contributes to this mind-set. Books and tapes and seminars promise the five keys to success, the eight principles of healthy living, or the single secret of healing. Some of these ideas are truly helpful, but they also feed into the notion that we can heal ourselves, if we only have the right catchphrase.

Yeah, right.

When we're completely honest with ourselves, we realize we need help. We finally recognize we have to reach out, that we can't go it alone.

This is a crucial moment, this reaching out. For many, it's the beginning of prayer. For those already pursuing prayer, it can take them to a new level of relationship with God. "Come to me, all you that are weary and are carrying heavy burdens," said Jesus, "and I will give you rest" (Matthew 11:28). God is described in many ways throughout the Bible, but one of the foremost facts about him is that he's a healer. He cares about our needs, and he assists us when we call out to him.

This book is about that healing process. It's also about angels, those supernatural servants of God who flit around the universe doing a number of important tasks. The Bible doesn't say much about the angels' own healing ministry, but it's clear that they carry out various crucial tasks that support God's healing work. Yet we can also think about people as "angels," in a metaphorical sense. We should be grateful for all those people around us who quietly assist in the healing process.

So you're not alone. There's a huge team of humans and angels who are highly invested in your healing process. Not to put any pressure on you or anything, but read on.

Do You Want to Be Made Well?

Healing: It's What God Does

The man couldn't walk. Carried by friends or relatives, he had come to the Pool of Bethesda for years, hoping for a miracle. Legend had it that every so often God would send an angel to stir up the waters at this Jerusalem landmark. The first invalid to get into the pool after the stirring would be healed.

Thirty-eight years he had been lame. We don't know how long he'd been coming to this pool—perhaps decades. But then something happened that changed his life. Jesus showed up and asked him a simple question.

"Do you want to be made well?"

Sounds like a no-brainer, right? *Of course I want to be made well, Jesus! Why do you think I hang out by this pool every day? Don't you think I want to get out and do other things? Yes, I want to walk! Yes, I want to be made well! Yes! Yes!*

But that's not how the man responded. He made excuses. "Sir, I have no one to put me into the pool when the water is stirred up, and while I am making my way, someone else steps down ahead of me."

How many times had this happened? He didn't say, but clearly the man was frustrated by the system. And you can't really blame him, can you? You wait a year or two for the angel to make something happen, and then it does—but you're just a little too slow. Miracles happened, but not to this guy.

The ironic thing is that he was complaining to the Miracle Worker himself. Jesus was dispensing God's power all over the country, healing people and casting out demons. Again and again, Jesus had shown his ability to make people well, and now he was offering this gift to the lame man by the pool.

"Do you want to be made well?" Jesus asked, and he got a lecture on why that could never happen. The man was focusing on the angel and the magical process of stirring up the healing waters, along with the elaborate mechanisms required to get into the pool first. A pulley system, perhaps, or several helpful weightlifters. But the Healer was standing right there in front of him, asking permission to make him well. It certainly wasn't what the man expected.

Fortunately Jesus wasn't dissuaded by the man's complaints. He simply said, "Stand up, take your mat and walk." And instantly, the man was healed. Of course he still had to take that literal step of faith, putting weight on those long-dormant legs, but he did that—and for the first time in 38 years, he walked (John 5:2–9).

A Curious Story

This is a curious story, one of the few in the Bible where an angel is said to participate in healing. After you read the gospels for a while, you get used to Jesus healing people, but it's odd to see this incident about the angel stirring up the water to bring God's healing.

Should it surprise us that God would send his angels to provide healing to invalids in ancient Jerusalem? Of course not. Our Creator has the power to heal, and he likes to use it. He can do that any way he chooses, with angels or without.

But this story also gives us a fascinating look at two different expressions of healing power side by side. The angel stirs up the water every once in a while, and the quickest responder gets healed. But then Jesus shows up, and he takes the time to converse with the lame man before displaying his power. There is a relationship begun here. It's not just some impersonal race to the water. Jesus sees this man, knows him, and challenges him to stand up. The man missed out on the angelic healing, but he found something far better: a genuine encounter with the Son of God.

Nowadays many people are crazy about angels. Some may talk about being healed by angels, and there's no good reason to doubt them, as long as one point is clear. The Bible assures us that the actual healing power comes from God. Angels are servants of God, and they have various roles—some of which may involve healing, as we see at the Pool of Bethesda—but they're not choosing whether to heal or not to heal, and the power they use is not their own. Asking an angel to heal you is like getting a hospital orderly to remove your gallbladder. We need to ask God for his wholeness, and he will choose the best way to operate.

But there's one more curious detail in the Bethesda story: Jesus asked the man for permission. *Do you want to be made well?* We think we know the obvious answer to that question (*duh, yes*), but that's not the answer the man gave. We're probably surprised by his answer until we realize that many of us have had similar conversations with God in our own lives.

Children learn early that being sick is a good way to get attention, not to mention a sure-fire way to skip school. *Oh, I'm so sorry I have to miss that math test, but*—hack, hack—*I have this nasty cough.* What if Jesus were to show up at our bedside at a time like that and ask, "Do you want to be made well?" We'd say, "Please, not until school's out this afternoon!"

On a more serious note, psychiatrists tell us that half the battle of kicking an addiction is developing the desire to kick. Sure, there are various substances that people get physically addicted to, and there's a period of detox that's necessary, but psychological addiction is a major part of the problem. Why do you think so many people have to return to rehab? The substance may be cleared from their body, but at some level they still don't really want to be made well. For many of these people, it's an identity crisis: *If I'm not a drug user, who am I? Please don't take my problem away from me. It's all I know.*

Jesus' question doesn't sound like a no-brainer anymore, does it? "Do you want to be made well?" He was asking the lame man to participate in his own healing, and he asks the same thing of us. Will we reach out in faith? Will we be willing to start a new life, free of the sickness that has defined us? Think of the transition that occurred in the lame man's life. After 38 years, he had to take up his mat and find a whole new way to live. You may have been ailing for 38 days, or 38 hours, but things will change for you when God brings healing. Are you ready?

Do not despise the discipline of the Almighty.
For he wounds, but he binds up;
he strikes, but his hands heal.

Job 5:17–18

It's What God Does

There's no need to be shy about asking God for help. In Scripture he tells us again and again that he wants us to do exactly that. "Call on me in the day of trouble; I will deliver you, and you shall glorify me" (Psalm 50:15). In fact, we often get the picture of God waiting for us to call, almost like a teenage wallflower sitting by the phone. "I said, 'Here I am, here I am,' to a nation that did not call on my name. I held out my hands all day long to a rebellious people" (Isaiah 65:1–2).

An actor auditioned well for the lead role in a musical, and he was pretty sure he'd won the part. He had worked in that theater before, and the director was a good friend. His closest competition at the tryout was a young guy who sang well but obviously needed some acting lessons. It was a shock when the director called to say he had decided to cast the younger guy. Disappointed as he was, the experienced actor was a team player and still a friend of the director, so he offered to serve as an acting coach for the guy who got the role. "Maybe," said the director. "I might just take you up on that offer."

But the weeks of rehearsal went by with no phone call. The veteran actor didn't want to nag the director, but he began to hope that he'd be asked to help. Oh, sure, there was some pain in losing a role, but he could gain some honor in contributing his expertise to the show in another way.

11

He really wanted to help. But the phone never rang. The show opened, and the actor went to see it, paying special attention to the performer cast in the starring role. As he'd expected, the singing was great, but the acting was horrible.

"Why didn't they call me?" he wondered. "I could have helped." Months after the show was over, he put that question to his friend the director.

"Oh, I thought that would be too awkward for you," the director said. "I thought you wouldn't want to do it."

Maybe you've had situations like that, where you deeply wished that someone would call for help. Maybe your kids were working on some project about which you could share some hard-won wisdom. Maybe a close friend needed your advice but wouldn't ask for it. You know what it's like to hold out your hands to people who feel that they don't need you.

That's often how God feels.

Of course, people have their reasons for not calling. It would be awkward. You're too busy for that sort of thing. Why would you care about a little thing like that? In the same way, some people assume that God wouldn't care about their little problems. But that's exactly what God does. He cares. He helps. He heals.

In the beautiful Psalm 103, David announces that the Lord "forgives all your iniquity" and "heals all your diseases."

Later he assures us, "As a father has compassion for his children, so the Lord has compassion for those who fear him" (Psalm 103:3, 13). In the New Testament, Paul puts it point-blank: "Let your requests be made known to God" (Philippians 4:6). No need to hold back. Peter echoes the sentiment as he suggests "casting all your care upon him; for he careth for you" (1 Peter 5:7, KJV).

You wouldn't keep yourself from taking your car to a mechanic because, "well, he's probably busy watching a ball game or something." No, fixing cars is what your mechanic does. He wants to fix your car problem. And healing is what God does. He knows exactly what we're made of, because he made us. He can get us back in working order.

Why Is Healing Necessary, Anyway?

If you tend toward cynicism, there might be a question gnawing at you. If we talk about God as a healer, don't we have to blame him for our problems to begin with? If he's so interested in binding up our wounds, why does he let us get wounded in the first place? Doesn't he have power to make our lives problem free?

We could discuss this question for a long time. Philosophers have debated it, in various forms, for centuries. This book focuses on God's healing, and how he heals, so we're just going to touch on this question briefly.

There's an odd story in the Book of Numbers that might help us. To set the scene: The Israelites had recently experienced a miraculous escape from slavery in Egypt that involved the plagues, the Passover, the Red Sea—all of that. They camped at Mount Sinai for a while and received God's law. Then they headed toward the land of Canaan, their once and future home. But when their advance scouts reported on how daunting the current inhabitants of Canaan were, the people lost heart and decided not to invade the territory. As a result, they had to wander through the desert wilderness of Sinai.

But God continued to help them during that time, sending manna from heaven and coveys of quail for their nourishment. He even defeated enemies along the way. But the Israelites grew impatient.

"The people spoke against God and against Moses, 'Why have you brought us up out of Egypt to die in the wilderness? For there is no food and no water, and we detest this miserable food.' Then the Lord sent poisonous serpents among the people, and they bit the people, so that many Israelites died" (Numbers 21:5–6).

Sometimes the God of the Bible seems harsh. This is one of those times. There is no free speech here. This is a powerful God dealing swiftly with rebellion.

But try to look at it from God's perspective. He has done everything he could for these people, even parting a sea to save them from oppression. He has provided for them and protected them. Why aren't they trusting him to continue doing that? In fact, they had an opportunity to enter Canaan, "a land flowing with milk and honey," but they chickened out. And now they complain about food?

It's as if they were saying, "Thanks, but no thanks. God, we don't need you anymore. We're better off without you." And God says, "Fine. See what it's like when I stop keeping the snakes away."

It's still harsh, but it makes some sense. Now let's see what happens next:

"The people came to Moses and said, 'We have sinned by speaking against the Lord and against you; pray to the Lord to take away the serpents from us.' So Moses prayed for the people. And the Lord said to Moses, 'Make a poisonous serpent, and set it on a pole; and everyone who is bitten shall look at it and live.' So Moses made a serpent of bronze, and put it upon a pole; and whenever a serpent bit someone, that person would look at the serpent of bronze and live" (Numbers 21:7–9).

The crisis caused repentance. The people recognized their error and prayed for healing. Compassionately, the Lord obliged.

One of the things that makes this story fascinating is that the Lord uses an object to bring about the healing. He wouldn't need to do that, would he? He could say the word and make things better. But he can heal in any way he wants, with angels and pools or with bronze snakes and poles.

He also invited the people to participate in their own healing. Just as Jesus asked the lame man if he wanted to be made well, God asked the people to look up at this pole in order to find health. (And given the size of the Israelite camp, some people might have had to travel a bit to get to where the bronze snake was.) Was there magic in the bronze sculpture? No. That would go against everything the Lord had been teaching the people. This was not a "graven image" to be worshipped. But it was a call to faith. People had to trust that God would heal them if they did what he said.

Jesus used this story as a picture of his own crucifixion (John 3:14), and it works vividly, but let's see the event in its own time first. The problems started when people were

The good Teacher, the Wisdom, the Word of the Father, who created us, cares for the entire nature of his creation. This all-sufficient Physician of humanity, the Savior, heals both body and soul.

Clement of Alexandria

blind to the goodness of God. Instead of being grateful for his provision and protection, they complained vehemently. And so God stepped out of the picture for a moment, allowing the slithering creatures of the earth to bring these people down to their level. The solution: Look up. Stop griping about the problems underfoot and look up to see what God is going to do about them.

So . . . back to our question. You are hurting right now, in need of healing. Whatever your ailment is (and you'll need to fill in the blank here with your particular problem—a disease, an injury, a broken relationship, a troubled mind), can you blame God for it? The answer always seems to be yes and no. Even if God hasn't caused it, he has certainly allowed it. Without getting too philosophical here, we can see that our whole world is marred by sin and rebellion, and we all suffer the consequences of that. Sometimes we suffer from our own rebellion, sometimes we suffer from the rebellion of others, and sometimes we just fall victim to the sad realities of a fallen world. In general, God chooses to let us (and others) make free choices—and to bear the consequences. Sometimes he steps in mightily to change things. Sometimes he's content to wait. At the end of time, he will set things right.

In any case, he has chosen not to make our lives problem free. If you're a parent, you can see the logic in that. Parents are often tempted to protect their children from any and all problems, but they soon learn that this is counterproductive.

The goal of child rearing is not to make their lives easy but to help them become good people. If their lives are too easy, that might not happen. People grow through challenge.

In the same way, our Heavenly Father allows us to experience suffering because he is growing us into better, stronger people. Paul says that we can "boast in our sufferings, knowing that suffering produces endurance, and endurance produces character, and character produces hope" (Romans 5:3–4). James seconds the motion: "My brothers and sisters, whenever you face trials of any kind, consider it nothing but joy, because you know that the testing of your faith produces endurance; and let endurance have its full effect, so that you may be mature and complete, lacking in nothing" (James 1:2–4).

This teaches us something about how to pray for healing and how God answers those prayers. He is a healer, no question about it, but he generally wants to heal us more fully than we realize. He is interested in our wholeness, not just a lack of sickness. Sometimes we become emotionally whole when we're physically injured. Sometimes we grow spiritually when we suffer emotional heartache. God doesn't promise to shield us from all pain, but to make us better people through the pain, to make us wiser, fuller, more loving, more attuned to him.

Renee was in her late 40s and single, two facts that she regularly bemoaned. At her church she led a Bible study group that had become quite popular with people half her age. Maybe it was her frank honesty, or maybe it was the way she cared for each person in the group, often calling them between meetings, but she had a cadre of 20-year-olds who were learning and growing week by week.

One night they focused on the issue of prayer, and Renee unloaded her heart. For much of her life she had been praying to get married and have kids. She knew she would be a great mom, and this was what she wanted more than anything. Yet despite her fervent prayers, God had not made this happen. It wasn't some serious disease she was struggling with, but she needed healing of the heart. To be honest, she admitted, she was perturbed about this whole thing. It was a grudge she held against God. She longed for a family, and he had not delivered.

Then one college student spoke up. "But, Renee, we're your kids."

The others nodded their agreement. "You've been there for me in a way my real parents haven't," revealed one guy.

"Just by watching you," said a young woman, "I've learned so much about how to live."

"I'm going to ask you to give me away at my wedding."

Over the next half hour, the group poured out their appreciation for this "mom," Renee. Her eyes welled up and ran over with grateful tears. The facts of the situation hadn't changed. She was still 47 and unmarried, but she began to see how God had been answering her prayers—not her way, but his way. By her faithful service in this church Bible study group, he had created a family for her in which she found wholeness and administered wholeness to others.

There are several promises in the Bible that seem to say we can get whatever we want if we pray in faith. Skeptics often cite these verses as typical religious overkill. "It doesn't work that way!" they insist. "I prayed for a mountain to move, and it didn't budge!"

But doesn't "faith" mean that we trust God to know how to answer us? The Bible also tells us that we don't know what to pray for, and that the Holy Spirit sort of translates our prayers (Romans 8:26). So maybe God listens beyond our words and into our hearts. Maybe he gives us not what we want but what we need. Maybe he does what it takes not to make our lives easier but to make them better.

He is a healer. That's what he does. He invites us to call on him with all our requests. We just need to trust him to use his wisdom to do the right thing in the best way.

A Prayer for Healing

Lord, you made me. You can fix me.

You put these corpuscles together.

You knitted my nerves.

You wrote my DNA.

You taught me how to laugh

And how to love.

Something's wrong now, the system's crashing.

I trust you to make it better.

But what does "better" mean?

Healthy, yes, but whole *again.*

Body, mind, feelings in balance,

Relationships in sync,

My spirit soaring with yours.

Lord, you created me and called your creation good.

Make me whole again.

Amen

Gabriel.com

Angels:
God's Messaging Network

She was terribly lost. Nineteen-year-old Charlotte routinely took a bus between her college dorm and the housekeeping job that paid her tuition. Classes, work, and the long bus ride made for a wearying day, and on this night, on the way back to her dorm, she missed her stop. By the time she looked out the window, she had no idea where she was.

The bus rolled on to San Francisco, 75 miles away from her college town. There, she frantically looked for help, but it was late at night by now. The information booth was closed. There were no police to be seen. A few unsavory characters were trolling around the bus terminal, and she knew she didn't feel safe asking them for help. She scurried to a ladies' room, knelt there, and fervently prayed.

A Bible verse came to her mind. "The angel of the Lord encamps around those who fear him, and delivers them" (Psalm 34:7). If ever in her young life she needed that deliverance, she needed it now. As she ventured out into the terminal, she noticed a young man carrying a big black Bible. Still too timid to stop him, Charlotte decided to follow him. This was crazy, she knew, but something seemed right about it. The guy looked like he might be a college student, too. Maybe he was headed back to her school.

He strode through the terminal, down one corridor, then another, and up some stairs, with Charlotte just behind him. Suddenly she saw a loading platform ahead of them with a bus displaying the name of her college town. The young man got on the bus, and she did too, but there was only one seat left, and he gallantly offered it to her. Then he got off the bus. She watched through the bus window as he took a few steps away from the platform and then . . . disappeared.

Charlotte got back to campus safely that night, convinced that it had been an angel who got her on that bus. Maybe you've heard or read similar stories from others—the guy who suddenly appears to pull a driver out of a fiery car and then vanishes, the flagman who waves someone away from a dangerous embankment and then can't be found, the mysterious pedestrian who shows up to fix a flat tire. Missionaries have heard from their enemies, "We would have attacked your headquarters, but you had that army of bodyguards stationed there." No, there were no bodyguards on the payroll. Those were protectors of a different sort.

Perhaps you're familiar with the story of the five missionary martyrs who died in 1956 at the hands of natives they were trying to reach, the Auca tribe in Ecuador. This was a courageous mission, and the tragic deaths made worldwide headlines. Years later, some of the wives of these missionaries returned to that tribe and found them amazingly ready to hear about Jesus.

But these women also heard a fascinating story. After the skirmish on the beach that killed the five missionaries, the killers heard singing. They looked up and saw a large group of people over the tops of the trees, hundreds of them, a hovering choir. It looked as if they were holding flashlights. This story was not told by just one person, but several. It had apparently been talked about, within this tribe, for years before the missionaries' wives returned.

Scoffers might try to find alternate explanations for all of these odd occurrences, but there's a growing body of experience in modern times that neatly fits with what the Bible says about angels.

So what does the Bible say? Who are these creatures?

Messengers

The word *angel* originally meant "messenger." Our English word comes directly from a Greek word, *angelos,* which carries the sense of "report" or "announcement" or of a person making an announcement. The Hebrew word for angel offers a similar idea, referring to a servant who does work on behalf of a master. All of this wordplay gives us a great starting point: Angels are messengers.

Angels came with a birth announcement to Abraham and Sarah. Though they were elderly, they were going to have a miracle baby. Angels entered Sodom to warn Lot of God's judgment. An angel appeared to Gideon to summon him into God's service.

These do not seem to be just heavenly gofers. They are ambassadors. Nowadays, if the United States is involved in an international incident, you can bet the ambassador of the other nation involved will visit the White House to speak (or answer) on behalf of that nation's leadership. That's the idea we get with angels. They are God's representatives.

The Christmas story seems to have an angel on every corner. An angel comes to tell Mary she will bear the Christ child and then shows up in Joseph's dream. Angels had already been involved with the birth of Christ's forerunner, John the Baptist, to Mary's cousin Elizabeth. Later, an angel (accompanied by a heavenly choir) gave the news of Christ's birth to shepherds and warned Joseph to flee to Egypt.

Angels reappear at the empty tomb of Christ, announcing the resurrection to the visiting women. They also accompany Jesus at his ascension, announcing that he will return. But they're not finished yet. One angel directs the evangelist Philip to a desert road where he preaches to an Ethiopian official, and another brings Paul a message of hope after he's shipwrecked.

In these accounts, we don't learn much about the angels—and that's kind of the point. An ambassador doesn't sit in the Oval Office and say, "I like jazz music, long walks, and I have an impressive baseball-card collection." Who cares about that? The ambassador is in the service of someone else. There is a message to be delivered. It's not about the messenger.

With this in mind, it seems appropriate that we only know the names of a couple of angels. Gabriel introduced himself to Mary by name, but most biblical angels are anonymous. Their messages, though, are consistently important. It seems that God sends angelic messages when he's about to act in a mighty way.

But it's also curious to note all the times he doesn't send angels. God himself spoke to Abraham several times, making great promises, long before he sent his angels for a visit. Exodus tells us that Moses encountered "the angel of the Lord" at the burning bush, but the conversation there is directly with God. Later we find Moses talking face-to-face with God at Sinai. There aren't many angel stories associated with David, yet we know he enjoyed a rich communication with God. The point is that God has many ways to get his message across. When he really wants to get someone's attention, he often uses angels.

Guardians

One of the most precious beliefs people have about angels is that there are "guardian angels" assigned to us, protecting us from harm. Many of the angel sightings we hear about in modern times involve a situation in which people are shielded from sure disaster. This idea of guardian angels is especially associated with children.

It's a great thought, but is there any biblical validity to it? Does the Bible really teach about guardian angels?

Yes. The idea comes through in a couple of psalms, and Jesus ratified it in the New Testament. The verse Charlotte remembered in the bus station, Psalm 34:7, assures us that angels aren't just a messenger service but are a security force.

An even stronger testimony to that effect comes in Psalm 91:11–12. "For he will command his angels concerning you to guard you in all your ways. On their hands they will bear you up, so that you will not dash your foot against a stone." This verse was actually quoted by the devil as he tempted Jesus, trying to get him to jump off the edge of the temple

I tell you, there is joy in the presence of the angels of God over one sinner who repents.

Luke 15:10

and force the angels to catch him. Jesus did not disagree with the premise of the verse, but he refused to put God to the test in that unnecessary way.

Later, as he taught about the value of children, Jesus said, "Take care that you do not despise one of these little ones; for, I tell you, in heaven their angels continually see the face of my Father in heaven" (Matthew 18:10). This saying raises more questions than it answers, but it does establish the idea of specific angels personally assigned to care for children. Jesus said these angels have a direct line to God.

It might help us to think about ambassadors again. Angels serve as God's representatives on earth, but here the idea is reversed. These angels Jesus talks about represent the "little ones"—children—in heaven. Perhaps those too young to connect with God on their own have heavenly helpers.

Yet it's not just children who are protected by angels. An angel miraculously sprang Peter and John from prison (Acts 5:19–20) and Peter alone on a second occasion (Acts 12:7–10). An angel closed the mouths of the lions with Daniel in their den (Daniel 6:22) and helped his friends withstand the fiery furnace (Daniel 3:28). The book of Hebrews describes angels as "servants—spirits sent to care for people who will inherit salvation" (Hebrews 1:14, NLT). Does it make sense then that angels might be involved in our healing? Sure it does.

Warriors

A foreign king was upset with the prophet Elisha. As the king waged war against Israel, the prophet always predicted his battle plans. The king's solution: Go get Elisha and stop him. So one day Elisha's servant went out for his daily errands and saw the enemy army moving into position on the mountains surrounding their town. "Uh-oh," he said. "What will we do now?"

Elisha was unperturbed. "Do not be afraid, for there are more with us than there are with them." Elisha took a moment to pray: "O Lord, please open his eyes that he may see." The servant took another look and saw that "the mountain was full of horses and chariots of fire all around Elisha" (2 Kings 6:15–17).

This was God's army, an angelic host ready to rout those who would harm God's prophet. As it turned out, they didn't have to use their force. God temporarily blinded the enemy army, and Elisha led them right to the capital of his own nation, where—surprise!—they were given a feast and sent home. They didn't bother the Israelites again.

But think of the lesson learned by that servant. He thought the jig was up for sure, but then he saw another plane of reality. Literally, he saw the angels of God encamped around those who fear him. The surrounders were surrounded. The protection exceeded the threat. That's a lesson we all need.

The Bible also gives us glimpses of angelic warfare. In the tenth chapter of his book, Daniel describes a conflict between an angel and the "prince" of Persia (probably a force of spiritual evil), with the archangel Michael coming to the angel's aid. How that battle was fought, we don't know. The book of Revelation teems with angels and with conflict. "And war broke out in heaven; Michael and his angels fought against the dragon. The dragon and his angels fought back, but they were defeated, and there was no longer any place for them in heaven. The great dragon was thrown down, that ancient serpent, who is called the Devil and Satan, the deceiver of the whole world—he was thrown down to the earth, and his angels were thrown down with him" (Revelation 12:7–9). Again, we don't know the details. Many interpretations have been offered. Is this a description of the original fall of Lucifer, or is this a future struggle at the end of time? Or somehow both?

Suffice it to say that, among the other things angels do, they also fight. Paul wrote about a spiritual struggle with "rulers" and "cosmic powers" that aren't flesh and blood (Ephesians 6:12). This is the conflict angels are involved in. The "heavenly host" that sang at Jesus' birth wasn't just a choir; it was an army. And it's no accident that at the first sighting of an angel in Scripture, he's holding a fiery sword (Genesis 3:24). The notion of spiritual warfare shouldn't strike terror in our hearts, because we who love God are on the side of the angels. Elisha's servant saw something

30

powerful and true. Angels are indeed an awesome force, but they're fighting for God and fighting for us.

Worshippers

Whenever somebody gets too crazy with intricate interpretations of the book of Revelation, just flip to the end and say, "God wins!" That's the theme. Whatever the bowls and seals and trumpets are, the important thing is that the vic-

A Prayer About Angels

Lord, open my eyes that I might see

A whole new level of reality.

When I feel surrounded by my problems

Show me your angelic army surrounding them.

Thank you for the tenacious way they guard me,

Keeping me from potential harm I may never know about.

Let me join my voice with theirs

In praising you, the holy one, the worthy one,

the hallelujah victor over all in heaven and earth.

Glory to you in the highest, Lord.

And peace in my little world.

Amen

tory belongs to our God. Revelation is not just some supernatural fantasy, some codebook, or some horror novel—it's a book of worship, and angels are right in the thick of it.

"Then I looked," wrote John, "and I heard the voice of many angels surrounding the throne and the living creatures and the elders; they numbered myriads of myriads and thousands of thousands, singing with full voice,

'Worthy is the Lamb that was slaughtered to receive power and wealth and wisdom and might and honor and glory and blessing!'" (Revelation 5:11–12).

John's vision is populated by "living creatures" and "elders" and "saints," and they all join in the singing at one time or another. After the war in heaven is won, we hear a hallelujah chorus. "After this I heard what seemed to be the loud voice of a great multitude in heaven, saying,

'Hallelujah! Salvation and glory and power to our God, for his judgments are true and just'" (Revelation 19:1–2).

This is one more part of the service of God. Angels carry God's messages, fight for him, and guard his people, but the Lord also likes to receive praise, and these angels are specialists. The psalms frequently invite angels to join in the worship of God:

"Bless the Lord, O you his angels,
you mighty ones who do his bidding,
obedient to his spoken word" (Psalm 103:20).

Isaiah had a vision of angels fluttering around God's throne on six wings, calling to one another:

"Holy, holy, holy is the Lord of hosts;
the whole earth is full of his glory" (Isaiah 6:3).

So it's completely in character for the angelic army to show up in Bethlehem, singing,

"Glory to God in the highest heaven,
and on earth peace among those whom he favors!"
(Luke 2:14).

In a way, this song wraps up the various angelic tasks. These angels were glorifying God in heaven, as they were created to do, but they were also delivering a message to earthlings. They announced that sinful humans could find peace with God. But in a way this was also a battle cry. The birth of Christ was the D-day landing, the beginning of the end for the powers of evil, and the angels rejoiced to proclaim it.

What Are They Like?

So far, we've been looking at the job description of angels, but what else do we know about them? What do they look like? Where did they come from?

There's some variation in the portraits of the angels that occur in Scripture, but we find a common element: brightness. When angels are described, they almost always shine in some way. They carry fiery swords or wear bright white robes.

Moses saw God's angel in a burning bush. When the angel arranged Peter's prison break, his cell was filled with light. Depicting the angel at Jesus' tomb, Matthew says, "His appearance was like lightning, and his clothing white as snow" (Matthew 28:3). Some scholars have suggested that light is the essence of angels' bodies, that just as we are made of protons, neutrons, and electrons, they are made of photons.

And what's the first thing we hear from most angels when they appear? "Fear not." That might suggest that their appearance makes most people cower in fear. Their brightness, perhaps their size, maybe an odd-sounding voice, as well as their sudden appearance—all of this could be rather scary.

They can also resemble humans. At Jesus' ascension, the angels are merely called "two men in white robes" (Acts 1:10). To Abraham and Lot, they looked like human visitors. The book of Hebrews urges us to show hospitality to strangers, "for by doing that some have entertained angels without knowing it" (Hebrews 13:2). They seem to fit in when they want to.

While most angels remain anonymous to us, we're aware of three by name. Gabriel appeared to Mary, but he is also mentioned in Daniel, as is Michael (who is also named in Jude and Revelation). Raphael is mentioned in the apocryphal book of Tobit. But those are the only names we have. Michael is called an "archangel" and a "great prince," implying that he has some standing in the angelic hierarchy.

Angels were created by God (Psalm 148:5; Colossians 1:16) as a special class of beings with intelligence, emotion, and will. There is no biblical support for the notion that humans become angels when they die.

Humans are called "a little lower than the angels" (Psalm 8:5, KJV), because at present angels are closer to God. But Paul says that someday "we are to judge angels" (1 Corinthians 6:3). We are two distinct groups, and apparently God has a distinct relationship with each group.

The Bible does refer to "the devil and his angels." A story can be strung together from various biblical passages and ancient legends: A great angel known as Lucifer exalted himself and opposed God. He led a rebellion that some other angels joined. They were all cast down to the earth, with a fiery eternal punishment awaiting them.

A Piece of Cake

Elijah had just had a mountaintop experience—literally. Atop Mount Carmel, he'd challenged the false prophets of the Baal religion and had won. The God of Israel was vindicated, and the false god was put to shame.

But that just ticked off Queen Jezebel, a major backer of the false religion. She put out a hit on the prophet Elijah, and he had to flee. After a day's journey into the desert, he crashed emotionally, deeply depressed, nearly suicidal. He fell asleep.

Then he was touched by an angel. Roused from his sleep, he saw a newly baked cake and a jar of water. "Get up and eat," the angel said. Elijah obeyed and then went back to sleep. And after another soothing nap, the angel tapped him again. "Get up and eat."

This is a ministry of healing, isn't it? Oh, the angel didn't zap Elijah's depression away. The prophet had to go through another 40 days and an encounter with God. But the angel was serving him, nursing him toward health, caring for his physical needs. This messenger of God was helping the discouraged prophet take the first few steps toward healing.

Angels can fly because they take themselves lightly.

G. K. Chesterton

Angels Among Us

The People God Uses to Heal Us

In the movie *The Pursuit of Happyness,* Will Smith plays a man determined to better his fortunes by becoming a stockbroker. He has a young son whom he ends up raising by himself while he tries to keep his head above water as he goes through broker training. It's an inspiring story of grit and personal dedication.

At one point, the son starts to tell a story he heard. It's an old joke—perhaps you've heard it—but it becomes fresh again in the mouth of this little boy.

The story goes something like this: A flood is rolling in, and a man has not yet left his house. A police car comes by with an offer to drive the man to higher ground, but he says, "No, thanks. I'm praying about the situation. God will protect me."

But the waters rise higher. The man has moved to the second floor of his house when a boat comes by. The would-be rescuers offer to ferry the man to safety, but he says, "No, thanks. I have faith that God will protect me."

And the flood waters keep rising. Now the man is on his roof. A helicopter hovers above him, and a ladder is lowered to him. "No, thanks," says the man. "God will rescue me."

Then the waters rise and engulf the whole house. The man drowns. He gets to heaven rather perturbed. He storms into the throne room and says, "Lord, I trusted you to save me, and you let me down! What happened?"

And the Lord replied, "Hey, I sent you the police car, the boat, and the helicopter. What more did you want?"

When the child tells this story in the film, the father is distracted. They're rushing somewhere, and you can tell he's not really listening. He may love the music of his son's voice, but he's not really tuning in to the story. And so the kid never really finishes telling it.

That makes sense, in a way, because the father operates in the mode of "God helps those who help themselves." He's not waiting for God or anyone else to rescue him. He's building his own helicopter.

But as the movie goes on, we start to see some kindness shown by those around him. He's working hard to get ahead, but he can't do it all, and he survives with bits of support offered by others—a doctor, an investor, a teacher, a church that runs a homeless shelter.

You might call them "angels."

Human Angels

We've been talking about healing, something God loves to do. We've seen that God heals minds and souls as well as bodies, and he uses many different methods of healing to do that. We've also been talking about angels, those servants of God who carry his messages, worship him, fight for his causes, and care for his people. Sometimes this care may involve healing.

Now let's expand our investigation of healing angels to include people who help in the healing process. Perhaps you've had someone do something nice for you, and you said, "You're an angel." No, the person didn't sprout wings or start radiating light. What you meant is that they acted in an angelic way. When they did something nice for you, they were doing God's work.

Jim was concerned about his old friend, Malcolm. Mutual friends had been talking about Malcolm's descent into depression. He'd recently gone through a divorce, he was diagnosed with an unusual disease, and there were whispers about alcoholism. Jim had called Malcolm a couple of times and left messages, but they were never returned. What else could he do?

Well, he could pray. Jim believed deeply in the power of prayer, and so he began praying daily for Malcolm. If this old friend was determined to sink into his depression, into his addiction, to wall himself off from everyone and wither away, maybe God would just have to work a kind of resurrection miracle. Jim begged the Lord to revive Malcolm's spirits, to renew his sense of purpose, to bring him back to wholeness.

After several months of praying like this but with no direct contact with his old friend, Jim found himself doing business at the company where Malcolm worked. Geographically speaking, it would now be easy to stop in and say hi, but emotionally it would be difficult. How would Jim be received? Malcolm had withdrawn thoroughly from all his old buddies. Would he resent a "sneak attack" like this?

When on a long walk, Jim often went through his daily prayer list, and here he had several corridors to traverse and an elevator to wait for. So he began silently launching his routine requests. Before long he got to Malcolm. "Lord, bring this friend back to life. Heal his heart and his body. Give him a reason to live. Let him know he is loved. Lift him out of his—"

He was interrupted by a voice in his head that was almost audible. *You do it.*

"Lord, lift him out of his depression. Give him power over his—"

You do it.

Jim began to realize he could be the answer to his own prayer. He wasn't any great faith healer. He wasn't going to lay hands on his friend and proclaim with spiritual fervor.

But he could say hi. He could try to inject some joy into his pal's life. He could let Malcolm know that he was loved.

And that's pretty much what happened. Walking down a hallway, Jim poked his head into Malcolm's office and had a pleasant conversation. They caught up a little but didn't talk much about Malcolm's problems. They vaguely said they'd need to get together again sometime, but they didn't set a specific date. Sensitive to Malcolm's withdrawal, Jim didn't want to push too hard, but he did convey a sense of friendship and support. He left the office with the feeling that a small step had been taken on Malcolm's long road of healing.

God Works and We Work

Ancient monks had a saying: "God works and we work." It was a way of putting together faith and commitment. We find it holding true today in the matter of healing. God is the healer, and we trust in his power to make things happen, but we also recognize that we ourselves can help the healing process in many different ways. We can and should pray for healing, but we should also note that we are often the answer to our own prayers. God frequently says to us, *You do it.*

This is not just another way of saying, "God helps those who help themselves." Instead, it's a realization that God helps those who can't help themselves, but he usually does it by bringing other people into the picture to help.

This is clearly seen in both the Old Testament and the New Testament. The people of God are consistently commanded to look out for the welfare of those in need. The Lord "heals the brokenhearted, and binds up their wounds" (Psalm 147:3), but faithful people are also charged with this ministry. It was assumed that sick people would find care within their families, but Old Testament law makes specific provisions for the loving treatment of people outside that safety net—foreigners, widows and orphans, those who fall into poverty.

The prophets regularly railed against religious displays that weren't accompanied by concern for suffering people. In Isaiah, God slams the false fasting of people who ignore the needs around them. "Is not this the fast that I choose: to loose the bonds of injustice . . . to share your bread with the hungry, and bring the homeless poor into your house; when you see the naked, to cover them, and not to hide yourself from your own kin? Then your light shall break forth like the dawn, and your healing shall spring up quickly." Note the connection God makes between his ministry of healing and ours. He goes on to say that if you "satisfy the needs of the afflicted," then the Lord will "make your bones strong" (Isaiah 58:6–11).

We find a continuity here. The worship of God puts us in contact with his love, which then emanates outward, through us, to those who need care. We praise God and then, in the spirit of that devotion, we do the work of God, helping and healing. God works and we work.

Elijah's life provides a stunning example of this tandem ministry. We've seen how an angel gave the prophet a hot meal. We know God worked a mighty miracle, sending fire from heaven at Mount Carmel. Elijah was no stranger to supernatural displays. But earlier, in a time of drought, Elijah depended on the caring support of a single mom. This woman was down to her last measures of flour and oil, but instead of feeding herself and her son, she made bread for Elijah first. God responded to this sacrificial act by ensuring that her supplies of flour and oil were never depleted. Surely God could have rained manna from heaven to feed his prophet, but instead he used the selfless ministry of this faithful woman. Along with God, she was doing the work of God. Elijah was the beneficiary of both a divine miracle and the amazing charity of this "angelic" woman (1 Kings 17).

The New Testament continues this approach. Jesus named "Love your neighbor as yourself" the second-greatest commandment, right up there with loving God. As we saw in Isaiah, faithful God-lovers are people-servers too. But Paul gives us an even bolder image: the Church as "the body of Christ" (1 Corinthians 12:27).

He used this metaphor to make various points. People have different abilities, just as our body parts have different functions. The Church is like any body in that way. But how is it the body of Christ? Well, what did Jesus do in his body? He taught, he loved, and he healed people. Now that Jesus had returned to heaven, his Spirit was embodied in the

Church. His people would now be doing the same works he had done. In fact, Jesus himself had said this at the Last Supper. "Very truly, I tell you, the one who believes in me will also do the works that I do and, in fact, will do greater works than these" (John 14:12). Sure enough, the Book of Acts records the ongoing teaching and healing ministry of the early Christians.

It's clear, then, that God wants his people to join with him in his ministry of healing. He works and we work. Together.

Natural and Supernatural

Are we talking about faith healers now? About people who get on TV with loud voices and bad hair and crazy antics? People who tell you to send in a handkerchief (and a donation) so you can get a divine blessing through your cable box?

Uh, maybe. We've already established that God can use all sorts of methods to heal people. Could he give some folks a supernatural gift of healing? Sure. That doesn't mean everybody who claims it has it. There are lots of frauds out there. As Jesus himself said about false prophets, "You will know them by their fruits" (Matthew 7:16). And self-promotion is not a Christ-like fruit.

But let's zero in on a much more common type of healing, something we might call "care." In the wide range of ailments, emotional as well as physical, we all need people who will provide moral and practical support. We need people to encourage us, to nag us to make a doctor's appointment, to drive us to the drugstore, to cool our fevered brow. Like Elijah, we need "angels" who can cook a hot meal and wake us up to eat it. Yes, we need professional doctors and nurses and counselors as well. All of this is part of the healing process. It all brings us back to wholeness.

When we look at the whole picture, the line between natural healing and supernatural healing gets blurred. It's all the work of God. Our Creator has built healing systems into our bodies, and he provides people with various skills to make that healing happen. So when a caring friend knows the perfect thing to say to get you out of a spell of depression, is that any less supernatural than the media preacher who implores you to "place your hands on the TV screen"?

Historians have long wondered how the Christian Church took over the Roman Empire. For two and a half centuries they were a persecuted minority, but they kept growing. How? Some scholars have found evidence to suggest that throughout the empire Christians became known as healers. If you got sick, your family might quietly seek out the Christian who lived down the street. That person might come and pray for you but might also provide some basic nursing care. In a time when people were running scared of epidemic disease, Christians were bold enough to show Christ-like care to those who needed it. "Bear one another's burdens," the Scripture says, "and in this way you will fulfill the law of Christ" (Galatians 6:2). Maybe God provided supernatural healing in answer to those prayers, or maybe he allowed the natural processes of cleaned wounds and fresh linens to do the trick. Either way, the people of that empire saw this healing and began to recognize the love and power within Christianity.

It's no surprise then, that in the centuries since, people of faith have always been at the forefront of the establishment of hospitals and medical care, especially in areas that need it most.

How People Serve as Angels

So if we can think of people as angels, doing God's work, are there similarities to the types of work that angels do?

Angels are messengers, and caring people bring us important messages, too. Some of the most important are messages of hope. When we're in need of healing, we wonder if

All night, all day
Angels watching over me, my Lord.
All night, all day
Angels watching over me.

Traditional spiritual

we'll ever be healthy again. We quickly lose patience with the healing process, which can create a downward spiral. We worry about feeling bad, so we feel worse. Our angelic friends can remind us that healing takes time and can keep setting before us the vision of our eventual restoration.

Friends can also give us perspective, especially when a physical prognosis is not good. When one experiences terminal illness, life-changing injury, or tragic loss, they don't need someone to blithely say that everything will be "all better" soon. But in these cases, the divine message might be one of wholeness. We need healing for every part of us, physical and nonphysical. Even if there's little hope for a physical restoration, we can find growth for the soul in these difficult circumstances. The message of hope might be a reminder of the heavenly joys that await us, or it might be a challenge to draw ever nearer to God in these remaining days.

Of course the message might be: "Get up and get going; you've been sick too long." Sometimes we get so used to ailing that we forget how to be healthy. Good friends can give us that verbal swift kick we need.

Scripture is full of examples of God giving people messages for others, messages of encouragement, challenge, and direction. This task is not just for angels. It doesn't mean that everything anyone says to you is a direct e-mail from God, but you probably have a sense of those people who have a gift of saying what you need to hear. Pay attention to these human "angels." Listen to them as intently as if a seraph were flooding your room with light.

We've talked about guardian angels, and that's another role our angelic friends can take. And not just our friends, but also the doctors, nurses, or counselors who care for us. We put ourselves in their hands, trusting that they will guard our health. We need for them to be vigilant with our vital signs, warding off infection, managing our medication and its side effects. But besides those professionals, we need those friends who will check in on us, who will go to the doctor's office with us or visit the hospital and monitor the care we're getting.

Often a spouse or other family member assumes this role, and the responsibilities can involve making meals, driving us around, or helping with some of the other practical matters of life. Depending on the amount of care required, this can be a tough job, and we need to be appreciative. Yet sometimes we make it even harder. Some of us just don't like being cared for, and so we resist the kindness of these helpers. We need to recognize that they are just doing what comes naturally. Sure, we don't want to impose on them, but there is something deep within these helpers that needs to provide care. They find satisfaction by helping us. The best thing we can do for them is to let them.

Of course angels also worship God, and there are people with this gift as well. They come into our lives and refocus our attention on the Lord. We might be moping about our pains and problems, but they turn our attitudes around quickly. Many people try to cheer us up, and there are some perpetual optimists who try to get us to look on the bright side of everything. Granted, these people can be annoying. But we're looking at something a little different here.

Worship is more than a positive attitude; it's a reconnection to God. When we come to worship, we turn our faces from our own issues toward the mysterious greatness of God. In Scripture, the angels sing about the eternal holiness of God, about the sacrifice of the Lamb of God, about the great victory he wins over the powers of evil. It's not all sweetness and light. It's not just a positive mental outlook. It's an encounter with the Lord in his awesome majesty; it's a commitment to a greatness we don't always understand.

So when one of these worshippers visits us, it's as if a window is opened toward heaven. The message is more than "turn that frown upside down." It's "God is doing something here. Let's praise him for it."

"Rejoice in the Lord always," wrote the apostle Paul, "and again I will say, Rejoice" (Philippians 4:4). Paul was in prison when he wrote that. The key phrase in that verse is *in the Lord.* No matter how bad the circumstances are, there is joy to be found in a relationship with God. We can be confident that the Lord has a purpose for us, that he has begun a good work in us and will keep at it. Whatever pain you have to go through, the Lord will sustain you. A few verses later, Paul writes about being content in any situation, good times or bad, summing up, "I can do all things through him who strengthens me" (Philippians 4:13).

In our toughest times, worship is not denial, but a push into a new dimension. That's what seems to happen in Scripture whenever an angel choir shows up. The world we know is transformed in an instant. Suddenly the air bristles with the knowledge of God. The whole universe is newly tuned to the frequency of our loving Lord. So when these people—these angellike worshippers—enter your life, let them lead you into that awareness. Worship with them.

Angels are also portrayed as warriors, fighting the powers of evil, and there are also humans who fight on our behalf. Let's tread carefully here, because people of faith are often led astray with talk of "fighting for right." We can get so caught up in winning that we forget about loving. The people we're talking about aren't just fighters, they're people driven by love. They don't shrink from confrontation. They go up against all obstacles, anything that would hinder your healing.

Your "warrior angel" is the person who calls the insurance company every day to make sure your bill gets paid, the person who respectfully but persistently holds doctors and nurses accountable for their treatment. Nowadays it's easy to get lost in the system, and if you're ailing, you have little strength to prevent that. Your warriors will work doggedly to ensure that you get proper care.

If it's some sort of addiction you're trying to heal from, your warriors will be your best and worst friends, because they'll hold *you* accountable. They will steal your cigarettes, flush your pills, or carry you out of a bar. Or if you've just grown accustomed to being sick, they may be the ones to get you out of bed and into the sunshine. They tend not to take no for an answer.

You can be grateful for the warriors in your life. They provide an energy that you may sometimes lack, and they can prevail on your behalf against forces of neglect, bureaucracy, or greed.

An Army of Healers

Maya had been fighting cancer and winning, but just before she started the final chemo treatment, she came down with a rare form of pneumonia. Her body was weakened by the

I have indeed received much joy and encouragement from your love, because the hearts of the saints have been refreshed through you, my brother.

Philemon 7

cancer regimen, and this disease rapidly threatened her life. It was a shock to her husband and children, and to the church in which she served.

On numerous occasions Maya had been a healing angel for others, and now she needed a whole team of them for herself. The people of the church jumped into action. One began calling people to attend a prayer meeting. Scores of people showed up on short notice, overflowing the small chapel. These "prayer warriors" begged the Lord to defeat this new disease, to give the doctors wisdom in treating it, and to give comfort to Maya and her family. Other helpers sat with her husband as he waited, offering encouragement, and still others cared for the kids. Some made meals for the family. It was a scary time for this family and this church, but it also taught them something about caring for one another. After about a week, the doctors were able to identify the strain of pneumonia and treat it successfully. Maya began to come back to health, cheered on by a church full of "healing angels."

There is an army of healers around you. As with angels, you might not know they're there. Some fight for you, some encourage you, and some turn your heart toward God. Like the angel that stirred up the water at Bethesda, some create an environment in which healing happens. Like Elijah's angel, some prepare hot meals and keep you from sleeping the day away. The Lord uses these people as surely as he uses Gabriel or Michael to carry out his work of healing.

A Grateful Prayer for Helpers

Lord, you've given me a great team of helpers,

And I'm exceedingly thankful.

Where would I be without them?

They seem to know my needs before I do,

And they jump to meet them.

I know you've given them those gifts of caring,

Of encouragement, of hospitality and healing,

But they're using those gifts as you intended,

To show your love to others—I mean me.

I am thankful to you and to them.

There's not much I can do to pay them back, Lord.

They'd probably refuse a reward anyway.

So I ask you to shower them with blessings,

Just as they have brought blessing to me.

Give them joy and peace in rich supply,

And let your love continue to flow

To them, within them, and through them.

Amen

Worship God, Not the Messengers

Angels Aren't God—They're Servants

The original hallelujah chorus is still ringing in the air. The triumph over evil has finally been completed. All that's left is the victory celebration. We're in the final chapters of the Book of Revelation.

John has been faithfully recording this vision, from the golden bowls of wrath to the battle of Armageddon, and now an angel comes to invite him to the wedding feast of the Lamb. You can imagine the sense of awe and wonder that must have been building within John this whole time. He falls down at the angel's feet to worship him.

But the angel says, "You must not do that! I am a fellow servant with you and your comrades who hold the testimony of Jesus. Worship God!" (Revelation 19:10).

What could be wrong with worshipping an angel? This was a supernatural being, a player in the divine drama, far beyond John in power and spiritual insight. It would seem to make perfect sense to bow before him, but the angel wouldn't let it happen. God is the only proper object of our worship. All of this prophecy from Revelation is about Jesus, the divine Son. The angels are only messengers, servants—"just like you," the angel says.

Crazy About Angels

This is a message greatly needed in our own time. People seem fascinated by all sorts of supernatural rumblings. Past lives, contact with the dead, extraterrestrial visitation, fortune-telling—it all promises to touch something beyond this world. People dabble in these pursuits, hoping to find some new wisdom about their lives, perhaps some direction or purpose. For some folks, it's angels.

Maybe this fascination starts innocently. Angels are in the Bible, after all. And it's greatly reassuring to know that these messengers of God are flitting around our world, doing God's work, protecting us, fighting the forces of evil. People gather angel stories, like some that have appeared in this book—accounts of individuals who have been helped by mysterious strangers who then vanished. We get a cool feeling—spooky and yet comforting. Angels are among us. Maybe we'll be fortunate enough to see one.

But somewhere along the line, we reach a tipping point. Our attention shifts toward the angels and away from the God who sends them. We turn our fascination to the nature of angels, their organization and hierarchy. Is there an angel assigned to our town, an archangel over our region? What are their names? What powers do they have? Maybe we even start praying directly to certain angels to help us in times of need.

The Bible gives us precious little information about the world of angels. We know a few names, and we can deduce some things from the stories scattered throughout. But there's a rich body of ancient legend and modern fantasy that can whet our appetite for angelology. You can hop on the Internet and find all sorts of people telling you how to contact angels, what to call them, and how to get them to heal you.

This craze is nothing new. It's obvious that Paul encountered something like it in the first century. "See to it that no one takes you captive through philosophy and empty deceit, according to human tradition, according to the elemental spirits of the universe, and not according to Christ," he warns one church (Colossians 2:8). Later he gets more specific: "Do not let anyone disqualify you, insisting on self-abasement and worship of angels, dwelling on visions, puffed up without cause by a human way of thinking" (Colossians 2:18–19).

In the Church's early centuries, a number of teachers tried to twist the root message of Christianity. Some of them gained substantial followings. One of these sects, which became known as Gnosticism, developed an elaborate hierarchy of heavenly beings, sort of a ladder up to heaven. Jesus, they said, was the first rung of the ladder, so the common Christian was just starting out on the journey toward God. Those who were "in the know" (*gnos* means knowledge) would learn to commune with angels and move upward to more and more powerful angels until they reached heaven's threshold. If you wanted a fuller experience of God, they said, you needed to get to know the secret knowledge of the angels.

Apparently ideas like this were beginning to develop in Colossae when Paul wrote his letter. That's why he emphasized the preeminence of Jesus. "He is the image of the invisible God, the firstborn of all creation; for in him all things in heaven and on earth were created, things visible and invisible, whether thrones or dominions or rulers or powers [and *powers* is quite possibly a term for angels]—all things have been created through him and for him. He himself is before all things, and in him all things hold together" (Colossians 1:15–17). Later he added that "the whole fullness of deity" existed in Christ's body (Colossians 2:9). In other words, don't go looking for something more or something better. The angels don't hold any additional secret. To get to know God, Christ is all you need.

The author of Hebrews starts at a similar point, building a case for Jesus as the culmination of the Jewish faith. Perhaps in response to a cult of angel-worshippers, the first argument holds that Jesus has a higher status than the angels.

"Long ago God spoke to our ancestors in many and various ways by the prophets, but in these last days he has spoken to us by a Son, whom he appointed heir of all things, through whom he also created the worlds. He is the reflection of God's glory and the exact imprint of God's very being, and he sustains all things by his powerful word. When he had made purification for sins, he sat down at the right hand of the Majesty on high, having become as much superior to angels as the name he has inherited is more excellent than theirs" (Hebrews 1:1–4).

The chapter goes on to quote several Old Testament passages that Christians applied prophetically to Christ. "To which of the angels did God ever say, 'You are my Son; today I have begotten you'?" (Hebrews 1:5; see Psalm 2:7). This leads to the conclusion that angels are servants, "sent to serve…those who are to inherit salvation" (Hebrews 1:14).

In the Roman Empire, the power of that point would be very clear. A patrician household would have servants, some of whom might be very close to the family, but they would obviously be in a lower position than the children. In God's household, too, the Son is higher than the servants.

Taken together, these passages leave little doubt. Angel-worship does not fit within biblical Christianity. It's a question that has been asked and answered. A fascination with angelic hierarchies may start innocently, but it threatens to take the focus off of God and his son, Jesus.

Obsess or Ignore

In his brilliantly witty *The Screwtape Letters,* C. S. Lewis presents a fictional correspondence between two demons, a novice and his mentor, Screwtape. It's delightful to get all sorts of philosophical insight and moral instruction in reverse. That is, if the demons are saying that something is good, then it is, in actuality, quite bad.

A Prayer of Confession

Lord God, I kneel before you, and you alone.
I'm sorry for the times I've mistakenly
Credited someone else or something else
For your miraculous work.
How could an angel, a preacher, a friend
Impart your healing power, unless
You were behind it all,
Inspiring, instructing, empowering?
I thank you for the ones you use
On this earth and in your heaven
To help me heal.
Lord God, I kneel before you, and you alone.
Amen

One of these insights goes something like this: Demons like it when people get obsessed with them, because they begin to fear demonic power and lose faith in God. But demons also like it when people ignore them, because then they can do their work unopposed.

We might make the same points on the opposite side of the spiritual battle lines. We err when we obsess about angels. As servants, they're all about worshipping God. They don't want to call attention to themselves. Maybe that's why they vanish when people look for them.

But we'd also make a mistake to ignore angels entirely. They do exist, and they're fighting a very important spiritual battle on planes we can't inhabit. Like Elisha's servant, we need to open our eyes and see this force mobilized for our support.

Attitude Adjustment

We ought to take another look at the attitude Paul addressed in Colossians, because it tends to creep into our lives when we least expect it. Not only were the followers of the angels wrong in their facts about Jesus (and about angels), but they displayed a number of prideful desires.

On a positive note, the Gnostics wanted a fuller experience of God. You can't fault them for that. It's a good thing to want to know God better, to desire a closer walk with him. But this positive impulse took some major wrong turns.

For one thing, they wanted to gain greater status with God through extra effort. You might call it a Faith Plus approach. It's embarrassingly simple to receive eternal life through God's grace—"not the result of works, so that no one may boast," the Bible tells us (Ephesians 2:9). But boasting is important to some. They don't want anything they haven't earned. And so they strive to climb the angelic ladder to God through their own study, their own discipline, perhaps a rigid regimen. The Bible reminds us that we are saved by God's grace alone. It is a gift.

The Gnostics also wanted to attain a secret knowledge of God. This desire might start out as raw curiosity, but it can turn into a dissatisfaction with God's revelation and an unquenchable thirst for the mysterious. We assume that God is hiding his true nature from us, and we feel the need to decode some heavenly cryptogram. Maybe angels hold the key, we wonder.

But those who do this are making things far too complicated. God is a revealer. He has given us the Scriptures because he wants us to know him. And he has revealed himself most fully in Jesus Christ. A disciple once asked Jesus, "Show us the Father, and we will be satisfied." Jesus replied, "Whoever has seen me has seen the Father" (John 14:8–9). They didn't need to get all other-worldly hocus-pocus about it. The answer to their question was standing right in front of them.

In that letter to the Colossians, Paul seems to make light of the desire for secret knowledge. To loosely paraphrase, he says, "Yes, there's a divine mystery. It's been hidden since the beginning of time, but now it's revealed. I've been preaching this secret. Do you want to know the secret? Here it is: Christ in you, the hope of glory" (see Colossians 1:25–27).

Were you expecting something about the ark of the covenant or the tetragrammaton or the angelic prince of Persia or the lost scrolls of Eden? Forget all of that stuff, because the secret isn't secret anymore. If you want any hope of participating in the glory of God, get Christ in you. Receive him, and the glory awaits you.

Finally, the Gnostics wanted to gain a mastery that others didn't have. This was clearly a matter of pride. The Gnostics looked down on the common believers, those who "only" trusted in Christ. They themselves were moving up to higher planes of existence, hanging out with the angels, tapping into the mysteries of the universe.

We still have that sort of thing going on, in and around communities of faith, as unscrupulous leaders prey on the insecurity of believers. Read my book and unlock the divine code, they may say. Pray this prayer and gain special access to God. Give to this ministry and join the inner circle of God's blessing. Insidiously, these appeals transform our honest desire to know God into a way to rise above others.

Of course the Bible confirms that we're in this together. We are a body, and every body part is important. We need to be helping one another to know God better, not jockeying for position. "Do nothing from selfish ambition or conceit, but in humility regard others as better than yourselves" (Philippians 2:3).

Down by the River

The prophet Elisha was well-known throughout his whole region. Earlier we saw how the king of a rival nation sent an army to get Elisha. In 2 Kings 5, we find that nation's leading general crossing the border to seek healing from this prophet. His name was Naaman, and he had leprosy.

The visit was a big deal—with official state paperwork and everything—and Naaman brought a bunch of gold and silver to pay for the miracle. When the general showed up with his horses and chariots, Elisha sent out a servant with the message: "Go, wash in the Jordan seven times, and your flesh shall be restored and you shall be clean" (2 Kings 5:10).

It was I who taught Ephraim to walk,
taking them by the arms;
but they did not realize it was I who healed them.

Hosea 11:3, NIV

This angered Naaman. Go jump in a river? Couldn't the prophet do better than that? It wasn't what he expected at all. "I thought that for me he would surely come out, and stand and call on the name of the Lord his God, and would wave his hand over the spot, and cure the leprosy!" (2 Kings 5:11). Besides that, the Jordan River was kind of muddy. There were much better rivers in his home country. And if it was just a matter of taking a bath, he could have done that at home.

Naaman started to leave, but his servants talked some sense into him: "If the prophet had commanded you to do something difficult, would you not have done it?" (2 Kings 5:13). That's right. His problem with the prophet's instructions was that they were too easy. His disease was far too serious to be treated with a simple dip in a dirty river.

As you seek healing for your ailment, whatever it is, be careful not to make the same error. You might be looking for some razzle-dazzle, some archangel of the third order who specializes in your type of problem, who can only be reached with some ancient prayer in the original Aramaic. If that's what it took, you would do it.

But the answer for your ailment, as for Naaman's, is far simpler. Pray. Ask God to heal you. Trust God to bring the assistance you need, in human or angelic form, to make you whole—mentally, physically, spiritually, emotionally—for his purposes. It's a simple approach, maybe too simple for some.

Oh, by the way, Naaman reconsidered the prophet's prescription, washed in the Jordan seven times, and was healed. The simple approach worked, because it was about God's power, not Naaman's, not Elisha's, not even the river's. Naaman submitted himself to God's simple way, and he saw God's power transforming his life.

Human Healers Get Worshipped, Too

A famous faith healer walked onto the floor of a Christian convention, and it was like the sea parting. With an entourage of about a dozen men in black surrounding him, he oozed forward through the crowd, wearing white. He had a best-selling book out, a video series, and a successful TV ministry, so a number of prominent publishers and producers stepped forward to pay him homage, and he stopped to shake their hands before moving on.

What's wrong with this picture?

If this man is truly a faith healer, then the healing power comes from God, right? Then the credit should go to God, right? And yet he has built a media empire appealing to people who essentially worship him.

This is a problem in our celebrity culture. We now have our own "faith celebs," the preachers and singers who have attained fame through their ministry, and we tend to put them on pedestals. As the angel of Revelation said to John, "You must not do that!" These ministers are fellow servants with us. Whatever power exists within their ministry comes from God.

This is not to say that all famous preachers, authors, or musicians are on ego trips, though that is an occupational hazard. It's hard for them not to start thinking too highly of themselves, because millions of people are crediting them with their healing, redemption, or spiritual growth. Feed the pride of such people for too long, and they can fall hard. Over the last few decades we've had more than our share of high-profile scandals among prominent ministers.

You've heard the old saying, "Don't shoot the messenger." It comes from the days when an army might send a messenger to an opposing camp with, say, terms of surrender. If the terms weren't acceptable, a hot-headed general might shoot the messenger, which was a bad idea—how would you get the word back to your opponents that you had rejected the terms? The point is that the quarrel isn't with the messenger. He's just a middleman, bringing the word from someone else.

We might tweak that saying to say, "Don't worship the messenger." If a preacher is delivering an inspirational message that lifts your spirits and sets you back on the road to health, great! But don't worship the messenger. The message is coming from God. Even if some healer lays hands on you and prays and your disease is miraculously banished, the power comes from the Lord. The healer is just a conduit of divine healing.

The same might be said for doctors, trainers, counselors, or even authors of self-help books. These people may play a major role in your healing. You respect them, listen to them, and do what they say. It's rather common, actually, to develop an overattachment to any of these healers. It will help to remind yourself that they are just part of the team that's administering God's healing to you. That doesn't diminish their skill, or the effect of their work in your life; it just places things in perspective.

It is good and right to be thankful for the effective, faithful ministry of those who inspire us, challenge us, diagnose our problems, and prescribe solutions. It would be wrong to ignore such people. (In fact, it might be a valuable exercise for you to list all the people who are helping you toward healing. You might be stunned at how many there really are.) But keep in mind that the healing power ultimately belongs to God.

Lift Up Your Eyes

The psalmist says, "I lift up my eyes to the hills—from where will my help come? My help comes from the Lord, who made heaven and earth" (Psalm 121:1–2). That's a favorite verse for many, but some folks have a slight misunderstanding about it.

Why does the psalmist look up at the hills? Many of us have assumed that it's a glance toward God, who lives up there somewhere, but it's actually a powerful religious commentary. Idols were worshipped in the hills, in sacred groves built there to honor nature gods. Sometimes people even worshipped the hills themselves, sort of a Mother Nature religion. But here the psalmist sees those hills and trumps them. *Does my help come from the hills? No, but from the Lord who made the hills.*

When you are ailing, it's important to look up. Get your mind off your woes, and contemplate higher things. But some people aren't too picky about where they look up toward to get help. Angels, stars, visitors from Mars. Whatever it takes. But fortunately the psalmist doesn't leave us in the hills. He specifies where the assistance comes from—our Creator God.

It was pride that changed angels into devils;
it is humility that makes men as angels.

Augustine

The Faith That Heals You

Trusting the Maker to Make You Whole

For 12 years, the woman had suffered with an embarrassing disease that caused her to bleed. She had spent a lot of money on doctors, who only made it worse. Besides the shame and the pain, the blood made her ritually unclean. She could not participate in Israel's religious life. Anyone who touched her became unclean as well. This wretched disease had stolen everything that mattered from her.

She must have heard that the healer was in town. Jesus had traveled around the whole region of Galilee with his offbeat teaching and his amazing exorcisms. People were saying he made the lame walk and he gave sight to the blind. She must have wondered what he could do—what he *would* do—for her.

What did it take for her to get out of the house, to push herself out the door? She had to get downtown to try to meet the healer, but she was taking a big risk. After all, he was a rabbi, a man of God, and she was an unclean woman. Would he even look at her?

Did she pray on the way, or was it just a continuation of the prayer she'd been breathing for 12 years? *Lord God, please heal me. I know you can find a way.* Did she perhaps feel the presence of angels at her side, helping her on?

As usual, there was a crowd around Jesus, and the woman must have fought her way through it. Well-wrapped, well-hooded, she surely didn't want to be recognized. But could she get to the healer? And if she did, then what?

She must have been nearly there when the synagogue leader appeared before Jesus. Eyes swollen with tears, the leader knelt before him and pleaded: "My daughter is dying," he said. "Please come and heal her. She's only 12."

Great! Now he's going to take off for this dignitary's home, and I'll never see him again, the woman might have thought. Who could blame her? She must have known her chances were fading. But then she knew what she had to do.

Her thoughts might have gone along these lines: *No need to bother the man. He's busy. But if I could just touch him, he could heal me.*

Jesus had started to walk with the leader, but the woman burst through the crowd and reached out for him. She just managed to touch the fringe of his robe. Instantly, she was healed.

"Who touched me?" Jesus demanded, whirling around.

His companions were bemused. "Master, you're moving through a crowd of people. They're *all* touching you."

"Someone deliberately touched me," Jesus continued. "I felt healing power go out from me."

Uh-oh. If the woman thought she could slink away unnoticed, she was mistaken. Trembling, she fell to her knees and told her story, from the onset of the disease to the jolt of power that had shot through her a few seconds ago.

Despite her fears, the healer emanated kindness. "Daughter," he said, "your faith has made you well. Go in peace" (Luke 8:40–48).

Faith Lessons

We can learn several things from this story. One lesson is of the Lord's impartiality. Jesus was willing to put the needs of this woman ahead of the needs of the synagogue leader, at least temporarily. She was out of the loop, religiously speaking, while the synagogue leader was about as far inside the loop as you could get. But that didn't matter. As it turned out, the leader's daughter died before Jesus could get to their house. But Jesus reassured the father and went anyway. Once there, he brought the girl back to life.

The second lesson here is a bit tricky: In this story, the positive energy of divine healing trumps the negative energy of uncleanness. The woman was ritually unclean. According to Jewish law, she had to be set apart so she wouldn't contaminate others. Healing her, making her whole, was a matter of destroying the negative energy of her uncleanness and reuniting her with the rest of the community.

That's not a crazy idea. In fact, it's rather brilliant, especially when you consider that this was part of the Jewish law about 3,000 years before scientists discovered germs. In the last century or two, we've all learned that health can be hurt by a different kind of uncleanness.

What we have here is a kind of showdown between Jesus' power and the woman's impurity. What will happen when she touches him? Will she contaminate him, or will he heal her? Of course we know what happened—healing. So wholeness, and perhaps holiness, is not just a matter of staying free from contaminants. It's about connecting with the life of God.

What does that mean for you, as you seek healing? Could it mean that wholeness means more than just getting rid of the disease? Is God calling you to a new kind of life, empowered by the positive energy of God's love and joy and purpose?

The third lesson we'll draw from this story comes from Jesus' sound bite at the end: "Your faith has made you well."

It makes sense scientifically. Medical research has established the value of a hopeful attitude in recovering from all sorts of maladies. If you believe that you will get better, you have a far better chance than if you don't believe it. On the other hand, if you give up, your attitude will affect your physical well-being for the worse. You can call this faith, and it can make you well. This makes sense.

But then it stops making sense for a while. Are we saying that you can have faith in *anything* and you'll be healed? Can crystals cure you? What if you put your faith in the reincarnated spirit of Harry Houdini? Could you just put your trust in your own grit and determination? The scientific answer is yes. The act of having faith in *anything* creates a lift of mental and physical energy that can help in the healing process. At this level, the power comes not from the object of your faith, but from the faith itself.

Yet that's not all that Jesus was saying to the woman. This was a 12-year affliction that was instantly healed. This wasn't just a shift in her attitude. It was a jolt of power from a healer who had displayed his power on hundreds of people throughout the region. It was her faith *in him* that healed her.

Are we saying that she caused the healing by having faith? Wasn't it Jesus' power that made it happen? Well, yes and yes. Her faith *accessed* Jesus' power. Faith is a lot like a light switch. The power is there, humming in the wires behind your walls, but you need to flip a switch to access that power and turn on the lights. In the same way, God's power is there, and we can access it by trusting in him.

A Prayer of Faith

You have the power, Lord, to heal me.

I don't doubt that for a minute.

You crafted me; you can re-create me.

I trust in your creative ability.

I know you love me.

You sent your beloved Son for my redemption

And you shower me with blessings daily.

I trust in your love, Lord,

Your desire to bring me health.

It's a little harder to trust in your wisdom.

I think I know what I want here.

I know what my healing will look like, sort of.

But how do you want to pull that off?

Seriously, what's your idea of my wholeness?

How would you like to accomplish my healing?

I'm guessing you'll want to touch my mind, my soul,

My attitude, my relationships, and—oh, yes—my health.

So let's do it, Lord.

I trust in your wisdom to heal all of me.

Amen

Healing the King

King Hezekiah was a good guy. As you read through Old Testament history, your eyes can start to glaze over with the succession of kings. Good king, bad king, another bad king, good king, three bad kings, good king, etc. Kings were graded primarily on whether or not they led the nation closer to God. Hezekiah did.

When his tiny nation of Judah was threatened by the superpower Assyria, he prayed about it, and God effected a miraculous outcome. The prophet Isaiah was a key advisor to Hezekiah. In fact, one day when the king was quite sick, it was Isaiah who brought some bad news. "Thus says the Lord: Set your house in order, for you shall die; you shall not recover."

Gulp. There's nothing like a prophet to tell you exactly what you don't want to hear. But Hezekiah "turned his face to the wall" and prayed about it. He also wept bitterly. "Remember now, O Lord, I implore you, how I have walked before you in faithfulness with a whole heart, and have done what is good in your sight."

We've all done that, haven't we? *I don't deserve to be sick, Lord. Look at all I've done for you!* In Hezekiah's case, it worked. Isaiah came back with a new message from the Lord: "I have heard your prayer, I have seen your tears; I will add fifteen years to your life."

Isaiah may not have been an angel, but he prescribed a poultice of figs to be applied to the infected boil that was causing the problems, and the healing occurred. Later Hezekiah wrote a song about this whole experience. He includes a description of the illness and his reaction to the news of his imminent death:

"I moan like a dove.
My eyes are weary with looking upward.
O Lord, I am oppressed; be my security!
But what can I say? For he has spoken to me,
and he himself has done it.
All my sleep has fled
because of the bitterness of my soul."

Then he realizes that his execution has been stayed. He will not die yet.

"but you have held back my life
from the pit of destruction,
for you have cast all my sins
behind your back.
For... death cannot praise you....
The living, the living, they thank you,
as I do this day;
fathers make known to children
your faithfulness.
The Lord will save me,
and we will sing to stringed instruments

all the days of our lives,
at the house of the Lord"
(Isaiah 38).

Here we see a man of faith dealing with sickness and healing, life and death. His responses are brutally honest. He
admits to "bitterness of the soul" when he thought he
would die. The thought that God was forcing it to happen
just made things worse. He found it hard to sleep.

Such feelings are not unusual for those with serious illness or injury. Many people become angry with God. Or
maybe they want to be angry with God, but they won't let
themselves voice such a sacrilegious feeling. Yet here we find
good King Hezekiah confessing that very feeling, and you
don't have to look far in Scripture before you find others
who expressed their honest—if not particularly pious—
emotions to God. Moses, David, Job, Jeremiah, and others
all join Hezekiah in that brutal honesty.

As in any relationship, you're not going to move forward if
you don't communicate. If you are hiding feelings of resent-
ment or bitterness, you won't be able to work through them
to get to a deeper relationship with God.

Once he realizes he won't be dying just yet, Hezekiah's
attitude takes a clear upturn. He expresses thanks. There's
something almost giddy in his teasing of the Lord—*It's a
good thing I'm still alive, because living people thank you—the
dead can't.*

Gratitude is a crucial attitude for us, too, even in the midst of the healing process. Thank God for the life you have, for the good days, for the people around you, those "angels" who provide the help you need.

Hezekiah also says he'll pass this on to future generations. Those 15 years mean extra time with the kids and grand-kids. They will need to learn about God's faithfulness.

Of course, we need to think about that, too. What are your children and grandchildren learning about God's faithfulness?

Praise the Lord: ye heavens, adore Him;
Praise Him, angels in the height;
Sun and moon, rejoice before Him,
Praise Him, all ye stars of light.

. . .

Praise the God of our salvation;
Hosts on high, His power proclaim;
Heaven and earth and all creation,
Laud and magnify His Name.

from *The Foundling Hospital Collection* (1796),
based on Psalm 148

Is your illness a source of anxiety or doubt, or are you modeling a more faith-based approach to your crisis? And if you don't have kids and grandkids about, then claim some. Find some younger person who needs your hard-won wisdom, and share it.

Finally, the last thing King Hezekiah decides to do is celebrate. He's going to pick up his stringed instruments (his guitar?), and he'll jam all day and night in the temple. As you recover from your ailments, be sure to schedule some celebration time. God loves it when we lift our voices in his praise—and not just our voices. Judging from this passage and several of the psalms, he loves instruments, too: guitars, drums, flutes, cymbals, and all the rest. Make a joyful noise to the Lord.

More to the Story

Hezekiah's story has two sad postscripts. Shortly after his recovery, he received a courtesy call from some Babylonian envoys. Now feeling at the top of his game, he proudly showed these Babylonians all the treasures in the temple storeroom. The envoys must have taken good notes, because when the Babylonian army stormed Jerusalem 130 years later, they carted away all the treasures Hezekiah had shown them. His pride hurt the nation.

The second bit of bad news is that Hezekiah didn't effectively pass on the awareness of God's faithfulness to his son. Manasseh, who succeeded him as king, undid many of the religious reforms Hezekiah had put into place. That's not necessarily Hezekiah's fault—Manasseh is responsible for his own actions—but it's still a cautionary tale for us.

Both of these matters deserve underscoring. Sometimes recovery from an illness can put us at a high point marked by personal pride. Watch out for this. If your trials have taught you to depend more fully on God, continue to depend on him when you return to health. Don't for a minute believe that healing means you've now got your own angels at your disposal.

Also, we all need to recognize that a serious illness or injury can rock a whole family. For a while, the energy of the whole household tilts toward the needy one, and sometimes important childhood needs can be neglected. Do all you can to express love and care for young ones even while you're sick, but especially when you've healed.

An outcast woman and an activist king, both hindered by disease. Both reached out in faith and received a miracle. See what God will do for you.

O Lord my God, I cried to you for help,
and you have healed me.

Psalm 30:2